AUTHOR BIO

Experience the culinary delights of Gourmet Vegan, an alluring plant-based cookbook that showcases the refined palate and love for food of its author, Georgina Heffernan. For those with a fervour for healthy and delicious home-cooked meals, this is the ultimate cookbook to add to your collection.

Georgina's decade-long passion for vegan and plant-based cuisine shines through in every recipe. As a former journalist, her love of writing seamlessly merges with her culinary art, creating an exceptional cookbook.

Nestled in Co Wicklow, Ireland, Georgina is blessed with an abundance of freshly grown organic ingredients at her doorstep. Her expertise as a professional artist has also been a significant influence on this cookbook, resulting in recipes that are not only delicious but beautifully presented too.

In her kitchen, Georgina has refined classic vegan recipes and added a unique twist, resulting in her tried-and-tested favourites. Her love for experimenting with fresh garden herbs, spices, and flavours has elevated the culinary possibilities of plant-based cooking.

Gourmet Vegan is not just about indulging in delicious food but also making ethical and environmentally friendly choices. By incorporating plant-based cuisine into our diet, we contribute to the planet's well-being and promote good health.

Georgina

Georgina Heffernan
Author

AUTHORS FOREWARD

Welcome to "Vegan Gourmet: Plant-based Recipes for Fine Dining." In this book, you will find a collection of delicious, healthy, and visually stunning recipes that will take your vegan dining experience to new heights.

Whether you are a seasoned vegan, or just starting out on your plant-based journey, this book has something for everyone. Gone are the days where vegan cuisine was seen as bland and unappetising. With the rise of plant-based diets, vegan cuisine has evolved into a rich and flavourful art form. In this book, I showcase the versatility and creativity of vegan cooking, highlighting the diverse flavours and ingredients that can be found in a plant-based diet.

 These recipes are designed to be elegant and sophisticated, perfect for special occasions and fine dining. From mains and salads to desserts and cakes, this book is filled with an array of delicious and visually stunning recipes that will impress your guests and tantalize your taste buds. With step-by-step instructions, detailed ingredient lists, and beautiful full-colour photographs, this book makes it easy for you to create gourmet vegan meals in your kitchen.

Whether you're a seasoned chef or a beginner, you'll find that these recipes are approachable and fun to prepare. I believe that plant-based diets are the future of food, and with "Vegan Gourmet, " I aim to show that vegan food can be just as delicious and satisfying as traditional cuisine. So, put on your apron, gather your ingredients, and get ready to experience the world of gourmet vegan cooking. Enjoy!

CONTENTS

PART I

MAIN DISHES

Part One offers a variety of delicious vegan main courses, including the Wild Mushroom & Thyme Linguine, Roasted Cauliflower with Truffle Butter, and Spiced Zucchini with Pickled Lemon & Harissa. These dishes showcase the versatility and flavour of plant-based cooking, and are perfect for special occasions and fine dining.

Sublime Wild Mushroom & Thyme Linguine

This is a delicious and comforting pasta dish that features the rich, earthy flavours of wild mushrooms. With a simple and straightforward recipe, it's easy to create a gourmet meal in no time. The combination of al dente linguine, sautéed onions, garlic, and mixed wild mushrooms, along with the addition of fresh thyme, lemon juice, and vegan butter, creates a sauce that is both flavorful and creamy. This dish is perfect for a weeknight dinner or a special occasion, and can be customised with the addition of grated vegan cheese for a nutty, salty finish.

Ingredients:

- 1 lb linguine
- 2 tbsp olive oil
- 1 large onion, diced
- 4 cloves garlic, minced
- 2 lbs mixed wild mushrooms, sliced
- Salt and pepper to taste
- 2 tbsp chopped fresh thyme
- 2 tbsp lemon juice
- 1 cup vegetable broth
- 2 tbsp vegan butter
- 1/2 cup grated parmesan vegan cheese (optional)

Instructions:

1. Cook the linguine according to package instructions until al dente. Drain and set aside.
2. In a large pan, heat the olive oil over medium heat. Add the onion and cook until soft, about 5 minutes.
3. Add the garlic and cook for 1 minute.
4. Increase the heat to high and add the mushrooms, salt, pepper, and thyme. Cook for 5-7 minutes, until the mushrooms have released their moisture and are browned.
5. Stir in the lemon juice, vegetable broth, and vegan butter. Cook for 2-3 minutes, until the sauce has thickened.
6. In a large serving bowl, toss the cooked linguine with the mushroom sauce. Sprinkle with grated parmesan cheese, if desired. I recommend the Violife Just Like Parmesan Wedge.

Enjoy your unique and delicious wild mushroom and thyme linguine!

Elegant Soba Noodles with Vegan Miso Cream and Roasted Vegetables

This vegan soba noodle dish is elevated with the use of unique ingredients such as vegan miso cream and roasted vegetables, which are combined with the traditional soba noodle, providing a delicious and original fine dining experience. The dish can be served hot or cold, making it perfect for any season.

Ingredients:

- 8 oz soba noodles
- 1 cup diced mixed vegetables (such as carrots,spring onion and mushrooms)
- 1 tbsp olive oil
- Salt and pepper, to taste
- 1/4 cup white miso paste
- 1/4 cup vegan cream cheese (vegan options by Daiya, Trader Joe's and Violife are all good.)
- 1/4 cup unsweetened plant-based milk
- 2 tbsp chopped green onions
- 1 tbsp toasted sesame seeds

Instructions:

1. Preheat the oven to 400 degrees F.
2. On a baking sheet, toss the diced vegetables with the olive oil, salt, and pepper. Roast for 20-25 minutes, or until tender and caramelized.
3. Bring a large pot of water to a boil. Add the soba noodles and cook for 5-7 minutes, or until al dente. Drain and rinse under cold water to cool.
4. In a small saucepan, whisk together the miso paste, vegan cream cheese, and plant-based milk over medium heat until smooth and creamy.
5. In a large bowl, toss the soba noodles with the miso cream sauce, roasted vegetables, green onions, and sesame seeds. Serve hot or cold.

Rustic Roasted Cauliflower with Truffle Butter

This dish is a unique and delicious take on roasted cauliflower, featuring the rich, nutty flavour of roasted cauliflower paired with truffle butter for a satisfying and decadent taste. The truffle butter adds a touch of luxury to the dish and the parsley provides a freshness to the dish. This dish can be served as a side dish to any meat or fish or can be served as a vegetarian main course.

Ingredients:

- 1 head of cauliflower, cut into florets
- 2 tbsp olive oil
- Salt and pepper
- 1/4 cup butter, softened
- 1 tbsp truffle oil
- 2 cloves of garlic, minced
- 2 tbsp chopped parsley

Instructions:

1. Preheat your oven to 425°F (220°C).
2. Place the cauliflower florets on a baking sheet, and drizzle with olive oil, salt, and pepper.
3. Roast the cauliflower in the oven for 20-25 minutes, or until tender and golden brown.
4. While the cauliflower is roasting, in a small bowl, combine the butter, truffle oil, garlic, and parsley. Mix well.
5. Once the cauliflower is done roasting, remove it from the oven and spread the truffle butter over the florets.
6. Return the cauliflower to the oven and roast for an additional 5 minutes.
7. Serve immediately and enjoy!

Pulchritudinous Portobello Pot Roast

This recipe is inspired by the traditional pot roast but with a twist of using Portobello mushrooms instead of meat. The Portobello mushrooms are rich and meaty in texture and flavour, which makes them a great substitute for meat in this recipe. The combination of the red wine and vegetable broth creates a rich and flavourful sauce that pairs perfectly with the mushrooms.

Ingredients:

- 4 large Portobello mushrooms
- 2 cups of vegetable broth
- 1 cup of red wine
- 1 onion, diced
- 2 cloves of garlic, minced
- 2 carrots, peeled and diced
- 2 celery stalks, diced
- 2 tbsp of tomato paste
- 2 tbsp of olive oil
- 2 tsp of dried thyme
- 1 tsp of dried rosemary
- Salt and pepper, to taste
- Fresh parsley, chopped for garnish

Instructions:

1. Preheat the oven to 375°F (190°C).
2. Remove the stems from the Portobello mushrooms and scrape out the gills with a spoon.
3. In a large pot or Dutch oven, heat the olive oil over medium heat.
4. Add the onion, garlic, carrots, and celery and cook for 5-7 minutes, until the vegetables are soft.
5. Stir in the tomato paste, thyme, and rosemary and cook for an additional 2-3 minutes.
6. Add the vegetable broth, red wine, and bring to a simmer.
7. Season the Portobello mushrooms with salt and pepper and place them in the pot or Dutch oven, gill side up.
8. Spoon some of the vegetable mixture over the mushrooms and cover the pot or Dutch oven with foil or a lid.
9. Place the pot or Dutch oven in the oven and roast for 1 hour.
10. Remove the pot or Dutch oven from the oven and let it cool for a few minutes.
11. Carefully remove the mushrooms from the pot or Dutch oven and place them on a serving platter. Garnish with chopped parsley.

Spicy Sesame Zucchini Noodles with Tofu & Edamame

This is a delicious and healthy dish that is perfect for anyone looking for a low-carb, gluten-free meal. With its combination of spiralised zucchini noodles, sautéed vegetables, and spicy sauce, this dish packs a flavourful punch. The addition of firm tofu provides a source of protein, while the edamame and red bell pepper add crunch and texture. The combination of soy sauce, rice vinegar, hoisin sauce, and sriracha sauce creates a spicy and tangy flavor that is balanced by the nuttiness of the sesame oil and sesame seeds. Topped with red pepper flakes and fresh coriander, this Spicy Sesame Zucchini Noodles dish is sure to be a crowd-pleaser and is perfect for a quick and easy weeknight dinner.

Ingredients:

- 2 medium zucchinis, spiralized or julienned
- 1 tbsp sesame oil
- 1 large onion, sliced
- 4 cloves garlic, minced
- 1 red bell pepper, sliced
- 1 cup edamame
- 1 block firm tofu, pressed and diced
- Salt and pepper to taste
- 2 tbsp soy sauce
- 2 tbsp rice vinegar
- 1 tbsp hoisin sauce
- 1 tsp sriracha sauce
- 1 tbsp sesame seeds
- 1 tsp red pepper flakes (optional)
- Fresh cilantro, chopped (optional)

Instructions:

1. In a large pan, heat the sesame oil over medium heat. Add the onion and cook until soft, about 5 minutes.
2. Add the garlic, red bell pepper, edamame, and tofu. Cook for 5-7 minutes, until the vegetables are soft and the tofu is lightly browned.
3. In a small bowl, whisk together the soy sauce, rice vinegar, hoisin sauce, and sriracha sauce.
4. Stir the sauce into the pan with the vegetables and tofu. Cook for 2-3 minutes, until the sauce has thickened.
5. In a large serving bowl, toss the zucchini noodles with the vegetable and tofu mixture.
6. Sprinkle with sesame seeds, red pepper flakes, and cilantro, if desired.

Sumptuous *Spiced Butternut Squash & Chickpea Curry*

This vegan butternut squash curry is packed with flavour from a blend of spices and the creamy texture from the coconut milk. The chickpeas add an extra boost of protein, making it a satisfying and nutritious meal. Enjoy!

Ingredients:

- 1 large butternut squash, peeled and diced
- 2 cans of chickpeas, drained and rinsed
- 1 large onion, diced
- 4 cloves of garlic, minced
- 1 tbsp grated ginger
- 1 tbsp tomato paste
- 1 tsp cumin
- 1 tsp coriander
- 1 tsp turmeric
- 1 tsp garam masala
- Salt and pepper to taste
- 1 can of full-fat coconut milk
- Fresh coriander for garnish

Instructions:

1. In a large pot or Dutch oven, heat a tablespoon of oil over medium heat. Add the onion and garlic and cook until softened.
2. Add the grated ginger and cook for another minute.
3. Stir in the tomato paste, cumin, coriander, turmeric, garam masala, salt, and pepper. Cook for 2-3 minutes until fragrant.
4. Add the diced butternut squash and chickpeas to the pot. Stir to combine.
5. Pour in the coconut milk and bring the mixture to a boil.
6. Reduce heat and let it simmer for 20-25 minutes, or until the squash is tender.
7. Serve hot, topped with fresh coriander.

Creamy Avocado Sushi Rolls

This recipe is wonderful because it's a vegan twist on traditional sushi, using creamy avocado as the star ingredient. The combination of avocado, cucumber, and red pepper makes for a fresh and flavorful filling, while the sushi vinegar adds a tangy sweetness to the rice. Plus, it's easy to make and perfect for a healthy and satisfying meal or snack.

Ingredients:

- 2 cups of sushi rice
- 3 cups of water
- 3 tablespoons of rice vinegar
- 1 tablespoon of sugar
- 1 teaspoon of salt
- 2 ripe avocados
- 1/2 cucumber
- 1/2 red pepper
- 1/4 cup of chopped scallions
- 4 sheets of Nori seaweed
- Soy sauce for serving
- Wasabi for serving

Instructions:

1. Rinse the sushi rice in cold water and drain well. Then, add it to a pot with 3 cups of water and bring to a boil. Reduce the heat and cover the pot. Let the rice simmer for 20 minutes or until the water is completely absorbed.
2. While the rice is cooking, prepare the sushi vinegar by combining the rice vinegar, sugar, and salt in a small saucepan over low heat. Stir until the sugar and salt are dissolved, then set aside to cool.
3. Once the rice is done cooking, transfer it to a large bowl and add the sushi vinegar. Use a wooden spoon to mix the vinegar into the rice until it's evenly distributed.
4. Slice the avocado, cucumber, and red pepper into thin strips.
5. Place a sheet of nori seaweed on a sushi mat, shiny side down. Spread a thin layer of rice over the nori, leaving a 1-inch border at the top.
6. Arrange the avocado, cucumber, and red pepper strips over the rice, then sprinkle with scallions.
7. Use the sushi mat to roll the sushi tightly, starting from the bottom and rolling up towards the top.
8. Repeat this process with the remaining nori sheets and ingredients.
9. Use a sharp knife to cut the sushi rolls into bite-sized pieces.
10. Serve with soy sauce and wasabi.

Enjoy your delicious and vegan avocado sushi!

Stuffed Smoky Aubergine Delight

This recipe is a fantastic dish that is both healthy and delicious. The combination of the smoky flavour of the paprika and the tangy taste of the balsamic vinegar, combined with the tender, juicy aubergine halves and the hearty quinoa stuffing, creates a dish that is both nutritious and satisfying. Whether you're looking for a vegan main dish or a side dish to accompany a hearty meal, this recipe is sure to please.

Ingredients:

- 2 medium aubergines
- 1 tbsp olive oil
- 1/2 tsp smoked paprika
- Salt and pepper to taste
- 1 cup cooked quinoa
- 1/2 cup diced cherry tomatoes
- 1/4 cup diced red onion
- 1/4 cup chopped fresh basil
- 2 tbsp balsamic vinegar
- 2 tbsp nutritional yeast
- Edible flowers for garnish

Instructions:

1. Preheat oven to 400°F.
2. Cut the aubergines in half lengthwise and scoop out the flesh, leaving a 1/2-inch border. Chop the flesh and set aside.
3. Brush the aubergine halves with olive oil and sprinkle with smoked paprika, salt, and pepper.
4. Place the aubergine halves on a baking sheet and bake for 20-25 minutes, until tender.
5. In a large bowl, mix together the chopped aubergine flesh, quinoa, cherry tomatoes, red onion, basil, balsamic vinegar, nutritional yeast, salt, and pepper.
6. Spoon the mixture into the aubergine halves and bake for another 10 minutes with a sprinkling of vegan cheese.
7. Serve hot, garnished with edible flowers if you wish.

Enjoy your unique and delicious stuffed smoky aubergine dish!

Herbaceous Pesto Pasta with a Twist

This Herbaceous Pesto Pasta with a Twist is a great recipe for those who love a fresh, flavourful, and healthy pasta dish. With a rich and creamy pesto sauce made from a blend of fresh herbs, nuts, and cheese, this pasta is sure to satisfy any cravings. The addition of sliced avocado and edible flowers makes this recipe not only delicious, but also visually stunning. A final touch of lemon zest adds an extra pop of flavour, making this pasta dish a winner.

Ingredients:

- Whole grain pasta
- Fresh basil
- Fresh parsley
- Fresh cilantro
- Roasted pine nuts
- Garlic
- Vegan Parmesan cheese
- Nutritional yeast
- Extra virgin olive oil
- Avocado
- Edible flowers
- Lemon zest

Instructions:

1. Cook pasta according to package instructions.
2. Blend fresh basil, parsley, cilantro, roasted pine nuts, garlic, vegan Parmesan cheese, nutritional yeast, and extra virgin olive oil in a food processor until it forms a smooth pesto.
3. Slice avocado into thin slices.
4. Drain pasta and toss with pesto.
5. Plate pasta, top with sliced avocado and edible flowers if you wish.
6. Finish with lemon zest and extra olive oil.
7. Serve hot and enjoy

Truffle Mushroom Risotto with a Twist

This Truffle Mushroom Risotto with a Twist is a delicious and hearty dish that is perfect for dinner. The combination of earthy and rich truffle oil, tender mushrooms, and creamy Arborio rice creates a flavour explosion in your mouth. The addition of parsley at the end provides a fresh and bright touch to the dish, making it a great choice for any meal.

Ingredients:

- 1 cup arborio rice
- 1 onion, diced
- 2 cloves of garlic, minced
- 1 cup sliced mushrooms (such as cremini, shiitake, and oyster)
- 1 cup vegetable broth
- 1 cup almond milk
- 2 tbsp truffle oil
- 1 tbsp vegan butter
- 2 tbsp chopped parsley
- Salt and pepper, to taste

Instructions:

1. In a large pan, heat the truffle oil over medium heat.
2. Add the onion and garlic and sauté until translucent.
3. Add the mushrooms and sauté until they release their liquid and become tender.
4. Add the rice and stir to coat the grains with the mushroom mixture.
5. Slowly pour in the vegetable broth and almond milk, stirring constantly.
6. Bring the mixture to a simmer and reduce the heat to low. Cook, stirring occasionally, for 18-20 minutes or until the rice is cooked through and the mixture is creamy.
7. Stir in the vegan butter and chopped parsley, and cook for a further 2 minutes.
8. Season with salt and pepper to taste.
9. Serve hot and enjoy the earthy and rich flavours of truffle and mushrooms, with a twist of parsley for a freshness and garnish.

Spiced Zucchini with Pickled Lemon & Harissa

This spicy zucchini recipe combines the vibrant flavours of rose harissa and red chili with tender zucchini noodles. The pickled lemon adds a tangy and acidic element to the dish, while fresh basil provides a fresh and herby touch. A drizzle of olive oil brings everything together, making this dish a quick, healthy, and delicious meal.

Ingredients:

- 2 large zucchini, spiralized or thinly sliced
- 2 tablespoons rose harissa
- 1 red chili, diced
- 1/2 cup basil leaves, chopped
- 1 lemon, pickled and sliced
- Salt and pepper to taste
- Olive oil

Instructions:

1. In a pan, heat olive oil over medium heat.
2. Add the zucchini noodles and sauté until just tender, about 3-5 minutes.
3. Stir in the harissa, chili and basil and cook for another minute.
4. Season with salt and pepper to taste.
5. Serve the zucchini topped with pickled lemon slices and extra basil leaves if desired. Enjoy!

Delectable Summer Rolls with Herbed Tofu & Pickled Vegetables

This recipe offers a delicious and healthy summer snack. The combination of crispy herbed tofu, crunchy pickled vegetables and fresh herbs wrapped in soft rice paper provides an explosion of flavours in every bite. This recipe also offers versatility with the option of adding a spicy kick with chili sauce or a creamy nuttiness with peanut sauce. Perfect for a light meal, snack or party appetizer, these summer rolls are sure to impress.

Ingredients:

- Rice paper wraps
- Herbed tofu
- Pickled carrots, cucumber, and red cabbage
- Fresh herbs (basil, coriander, mint)
- Spicy chili sauce
- Peanut sauce

Instructions:

1. Prepare the herbed tofu by marinating sliced tofu in a mixture of olive oil, garlic, and fresh herbs. Bake in the oven until crispy.
2. Pickle the carrots, cucumber, and red cabbage by mixing with vinegar, sugar, salt, and spices.
3. Dip the rice paper wraps in warm water for 10 seconds and place on a clean surface.
4. Place a few slices of herbed tofu on the centre of each wrap.
5. Top with a few spoonful's of the pickled vegetables and fresh herbs.
6. Roll up the wraps, tucking in the sides as you go.
7. Serve with spicy chili sauce and peanut sauce for dipping.Yummy!

Pomegranate and Nut Encrusted Tofu

This dish is a fine dining vegan recipe that is both sophisticated and delicious. The pomegranate and nut coating adds a unique and flavorful crunch to the tofu, while the spicy peanut dip adds a tangy contrast.

Ingredients:

- 1 block of firm tofu, pressed and cut into 1 inch cubes
- 1/2 cup pomegranate seeds
- 1/4 cup chopped mixed nuts (such as almonds, pecans, and walnuts)
- 2 tbsp panko breadcrumbs
- 1 tbsp nutritional yeast
- 1 tsp smoked paprika
- Salt and pepper, to taste
- 1/4 cup all-purpose flour
- 1 tbsp cornstarch
- 1/4 cup unsweetened non-dairy milk
- 1 tbsp olive oil
- 1 tbsp maple syrup
- 1 tbsp soy sauce
- 1 tsp rice vinegar
- 1/4 cup pomegranate juice
- 1 tbsp cornstarch
- 1 tbsp water

Instructions:

1. Preheat your oven to 375°F (190°C).
2. In a food processor, pulse the pomegranate seeds, nuts, breadcrumbs, nutritional yeast, smoked paprika, and a pinch of salt and pepper until it becomes a coarse paste.
3. In a shallow dish, mix together the flour and cornstarch. In another shallow dish, mix together the non-dairy milk, olive oil, maple syrup, soy sauce, and rice vinegar.
4. Dip the tofu cubes in the flour mixture, then the non-dairy milk mixture, then press the tofu cubes in the pomegranate seed and nut mixture to coat.
5. Place the tofu cubes on a parchment-lined baking sheet and bake for 20-25 minutes, or until golden brown and crispy.
6. While the tofu is baking, make the pomegranate reduction. Create a small platter adding a simple peanut dipping sauce to taste.
7. Serve the tofu cubes over a bed of quinoa or brown rice, and top with the pomegranate seeds for drama.

Gourmet Vegan Burger

This recipe for Gourmet with a Twist features a patty made from mashed chickpeas, quinoa, and breadcrumbs, seasoned with nutritional yeast, soy sauce, paprika, cumin, garlic powder, and black pepper. The patties are then cooked to golden brown in a skillet and served on a toasted bun with avocado, tomato, red onion, and lettuce. This delicious and healthy burger is sure to be a hit among vegans!

Ingredients:

- 1 1/2 cups cooked chickpeas, mashed
- 1/2 cup cooked quinoa
- 1/4 cup breadcrumbs
- 2 tbsp nutritional yeast
- 1 tbsp soy sauce
- 1 tsp paprika
- 1 tsp cumin
- 1/2 tsp garlic powder
- 1/4 tsp black pepper
- 1 large avocado, mashed
- 1 large tomato, sliced
- 1/4 cup red onion, sliced
- 4 buns of your choice
- 4 lettuce leaves

Instructions:

1. In a large bowl, mix together chickpeas, quinoa, breadcrumbs, nutritional yeast, soy sauce, paprika, cumin, garlic powder, and black pepper until well combined.
2. Shape the mixture into 4 equal patties.
3. Heat a large skillet over medium-high heat and cook the patties for 3-4 minutes on each side, or until golden brown.
4. Toast the buns in a toaster or on the skillet.
5. Assemble the burgers by spreading avocado on the bottom of each bun, then placing a patty on top, followed by a tomato slice and red onion.
6. Serve with a lettuce leaf and enjoy!

Cajun Spiced Jackfruit Tacos

This recipe for Cajun Spiced Jackfruit Tacos is a delicious twist on traditional tacos and one of my favourites for summer dining in my garden. The jackfruit is drained and shredded to mimic the texture of meat, then cooked with Cajun seasoning for a spicy and smoky flavour. The diced onion and garlic add depth to the dish, while the avocado, cilantro, and lime wedges bring freshness to the tacos. These easy-to-make tacos are perfect for a quick and flavourful vegan meal.

Ingredients:

- 1 can jackfruit, drained and shredded
- 2 tbsp olive oil
- 1 onion, diced
- 2 cloves of garlic, minced
- 2 tsp Cajun seasoning
- Salt and pepper, to taste
- 8 corn tortillas
- Toppings: diced avocado, cilantro, lime wedges

Instructions:

1. In a large skillet, heat the olive oil over medium heat.
2. Add the onion and garlic and sauté until translucent.
3. Add the shredded jackfruit and Cajun seasoning. Stir to coat the jackfruit evenly.
4. Season with salt and pepper to taste.
5. Sauté until the jackfruit is heated through and has a slightly crispy texture.
6. Heat the tortillas in a dry skillet or over an open flame until slightly charred.
7. Assemble the tacos by placing a few spoonful's of the jackfruit mixture on a tortilla, and then topping with diced avocado, sweetcorn, cilantro, and a squeeze of lime juice.
8. Serve hot and enjoy!

Spicy Southwest Avocado Toast

This recipe adds a spicy twist to the classic avocado toast by incorporating cayenne pepper and diced jalapeño pepper, as well as a variety of colourful vegetables for added flavour and nutrition. The coriander and lime juice also add a fresh and bright taste. This dish is perfect for a unique and sophisticated vegan breakfast option.

Ingredients:

- 2 ripe avocados
- 1 lime, juiced
- 1/2 teaspoon cayenne pepper
- Salt and pepper, to taste
- 4 slices of whole grain bread
- 1/4 cup chopped coriander
- 1/4 cup chopped red onion
- 1/4 cup diced tomatoes
- 1/4 cup diced bell pepper
- 1/4 cup diced jalapeño pepper
- 1 tablespoon olive oil

Instructions:

1. In a small bowl, mash the avocados with the lime juice, cayenne pepper, salt, and pepper.
2. Toast the bread slices.
3. Spread the avocado mixture evenly on the toasted bread slices.
4. In a separate small pan, heat the olive oil over medium heat. Add the cilantro, red onion, tomatoes, bell pepper, and jalapeño pepper. Cook for 5-7 minutes or until vegetables are slightly softened.
5. Top the avocado toast with the vegetable mixture.
6. Serve and enjoy!

Artisan Vegan Sausage

These sausages are a great alternative for vegans who miss the taste and texture of traditional sausages. The combination of sweet potato and cannellini beans provides a meaty texture, while the seasoning and spices give it a delicious gourmet flavour.

Ingredients:

- 1 cup cooked and mashed sweet potato
- 1 cup cooked and mashed cannellini beans
- 1 cup vital wheat gluten
- 2 tbsp nutritional yeast
- 1 tbsp olive oil
- 2 tbsp tomato paste
- 1 tbsp smoked paprika
- 1 tsp fennel seed
- 1 tsp dried thyme
- Salt and pepper, to taste

Instructions:

1. In a large mixing bowl, combine sweet potato, cannellini beans, vital wheat gluten, nutritional yeast, olive oil, tomato paste, smoked paprika, fennel seed, thyme, salt, and pepper. Mix until well combined.
2. Knead the mixture for a couple of minutes until it becomes firm and elastic.
3. Divide the dough into 8 equal portions and shape them into sausage shapes.
4. Place sausages on a baking sheet lined with parchment paper.
5. Steam the sausages for 30 minutes.
6. Once steamed, sausages can be grilled or pan-fried until crispy.

Deconstructed Pomodoro Pasta

This pasta dish is a deconstructed version of the classic pasta pomodoro, where the cherry tomatoes are cooked down to a sauce. The burst cherry tomatoes give the dish a fresh, bright flavour and a nice texture. This dish can be served as a main course or as a side dish.

Ingredients:

- 8 oz spaghetti
- 2 tbsp olive oil
- 1 onion, diced
- 2 cloves of garlic, minced
- 2 cups cherry tomatoes
- 1/4 cup fresh basil leaves
- Salt and pepper, to taste

Instructions:

1. Cook the spaghetti according to package instructions. Drain and set aside
2. In a large skillet, heat the olive oil over medium heat
3. Add the onion and garlic and sauté until translucent
4. Add the cherry tomatoes and sauté until they start to burst and release their juices
5. Remove the skillet from heat and use a fork to gently burst the tomatoes
6. Toss the spaghetti with the tomato sauce and basil
7. Season with salt and pepper to taste
8. Plate the spaghetti and top with fresh basil leaves

Enticing Vegan Pizza with Cashew Mozzarella

This recipe is for a delicious and healthy vegan pizza made with a cashew mozzarella cheese. The cashew mozzarella is made by blending soaked cashews with nutritional yeast, lemon juice, salt and water until smooth, then spread over the pizza crust. Top the cheese with a tomato sauce and your favourite toppings, and bake for 15-20 minutes for a crispy and satisfying meal. The cashew mozzarella provides a creamy and flavourful cheese alternative, making this pizza suitable for vegans and those with dairy allergies.

Ingredients:

- 1 lb pizza dough
- 1/2 cup tomato sauce
- 1 tbsp olive oil
- 2 cloves of garlic, minced
- Salt and pepper, to taste
- 1 cup cashew mozzarella (see recipe below)
- Assorted toppings of your choice (e.g . asparagus, artichoke, fresh basil)

For the Cashew Mozzarella:

- 1 cup raw cashews, soaked for at least 4 hours
- 1/4 cup nutritional yeast
- 1 tbsp lemon juice
- 1 tsp salt
- 1/2 cup water

Instructions:

1. Preheat the oven to 425 degrees F.
2. Roll out the pizza dough to your desired thickness and place it on a baking sheet or pizza stone.
3. In a small bowl, mix together the tomato sauce, olive oil, garlic, salt and pepper. Spread the mixture over the dough.
4. To make the cashew mozzarella, drain and rinse the soaked cashews, then add them to a blender with the nutritional yeast, lemon juice, salt and water. Blend until smooth.
5. Spread the cashew mozzarella over the pizza dough, leaving a small border for the crust.
6. Add your desired toppings, then transfer the pizza to the oven and bake for 15-20 minutes, or until the crust is golden and crispy.
7. Let the pizza cool for a few minutes before slicing and serving.

Elevated Vegan Chili Sin Carne

This vegan Chili Sin Carne is a hearty and satisfying dish that is perfect for a cold winter night. The combination of mushrooms and seitan or plant-based ground meat gives the chili a meaty texture and depth of flavour, while the red kidney beans provide a filling and satisfying base. This recipe is easy to make, and you can always add more or less spice to suit your taste.

Ingredients:

- 2 tbsp olive oil
- 1 onion, diced
- 2 cloves of garlic, minced
- 1 cup diced cremini mushrooms
- 1 cup diced seitan or plant-based ground meat
- 2 cans of red kidney beans, drained and rinsed
- 1 can diced tomatoes
- 2 tbsp tomato paste
- 1 tbsp chili powder
- 2 tsp ground cumin
- 1 tsp smoked paprika
- Salt and pepper, to taste

Instructions:

1. In a large pot or Dutch oven, heat the olive oil over medium heat.
2. Add the onion and garlic and sauté until translucent.
3. Add the mushrooms and sauté until they release their liquid and become tender.
4. Stir in the seitan or plant-based ground meat, and cook until browned.
5. Add the red kidney beans, diced tomatoes, tomato paste, chili powder, cumin, smoked paprika, salt, and pepper. Stir to combine.
6. Bring the mixture to a simmer and reduce the heat to low. Cook for 30-40 minutes, or until the sauce has thickened and the flavours have melded together.
7. Serve hot with toppings such as vegan sour cream, or chopped red cabbage.

Opulent Pad Thai with Crisp Pan-Fried Tofu and Peanut Sauce

This dish is a delicious and original take on traditional Pad Thai, featuring the classic flavours of peanut sauce, mixed vegetables, and crispy pan-fried tofu. The rice vinegar and brown sugar add a sweet and tangy flavour to the dish and the lime juice adds a freshness to the dish. The peanuts and coriander add a nice crunch and freshness to the dish. This dish can be served as a main course for lunch or dinner.

Ingredients:

- 8 oz of Rice noodles
- 1 block of firm tofu, pressed and diced
- 2 tbsp vegetable oil
- Salt and pepper
- 2 cloves of garlic, minced
- 1/4 cup vegetable broth
- 2 tbsp soy sauce
- 2 tbsp rice vinegar
- 2 tbsp brown sugar
- 2 tbsp peanut butter
- 1 tbsp lime juice
- 2 cups of mixed vegetables (such as bell peppers, carrots, bean sprouts and scallions)
- 1/4 cup chopped peanuts
- 1/4 cup chopped coriander
- Lime wedges for serving

Instructions:

1. Soak the rice noodles in hot water for 10 minutes or until softened. Drain and set aside.
2. In a large skillet or wok, heat 1 tbsp of oil over medium-high heat. Add the tofu and season with salt and pepper. Cook for about 5-7 minutes or until crispy and golden brown. Remove from skillet and set aside.
3. In the same skillet, heat the remaining 1 tbsp of oil over medium-high heat. Add the garlic and sauté for 1 minute.
4. Add the vegetables and sauté for 2-3 minutes or until they are tender.
5. In a small bowl, mix together the broth, soy sauce, rice vinegar, brown sugar, peanut butter, and lime juice to make the sauce.
6. Add the sauce to the skillet and bring to a simmer.
7. Add the cooked noodles and toss until they are coated with the sauce.
8. Add the crispy tofu and toss until everything is well combined.
9. Garnish with chopped peanuts and coriander and serve with lime wedges on the side.

Fusion Vegan Ramen Bowl

This vegan fusion ramen bowl is a delicious and flavourful meal that is easy to make and perfect for lunch or dinner. With its aromatic broth made from shiitake mushrooms, carrots, bok choy, bell peppers, and spices, this dish is both nourishing and satisfying. The noodles are cooked to perfection, and the broth is rich, savoury and perfect for a cold day. Topped with scallions, cilantro, sesame oil, and chili flakes, this ramen bowl is a feast for the senses.

Ingredients:

- 4 packs of Ramen noodles
- 4 cups vegetable broth
- 2 cups of sliced shiitake mushrooms
- 1 cup sliced carrots
- 1 cup sliced bok choy
- 1 cup sliced bell peppers
- 2 tbsp soy sauce
- 2 tbsp mirin
- 2 tbsp miso paste
- 1 tbsp grated ginger
- 1 tbsp grated garlic
- 1/4 cup chopped scallions
- 1/4 cup chopped coriander
- Sriracha or chili flakes, to taste
- Sesame oil, for garnish

Instructions:

1. In a large pot, bring the vegetable broth to a boil.
2. Add the shiitake mushrooms, carrots, bok choy, bell peppers, soy sauce, mirin, miso paste, ginger and garlic.
3. Reduce the heat and let it simmer for about 15 minutes.
4. In a separate pot, cook the ramen noodles according to package instructions. Drain and set aside.
5. Once the broth is ready, adjust the seasoning if needed.
6. Serve the ramen noodles in bowls and ladle the broth over the top.
7. Garnish with chopped scallions, coriander, and a drizzle of sesame oil. Add sriracha or chili flakes to taste. Decorate with a slice of lime

Five- Star Falafel with Caramelized Onion Relish

This Falafel recipe is a quick, healthy, and delicious plant-based dish. Chickpeas, herbs, spices, and onions are blended, fried to golden crisp, and topped with a sweet and tangy caramelized onion relish. Serve with hummus or a green salad for a complete meal

Ingredients:

Falafel:
- 1 cup dried chickpeas, soaked overnight and drained
- 1/2 cup chopped parsley
- 1/2 cup chopped coriander
- 2 cloves of garlic
- 1 small onion, chopped
- 1 tsp cumin powder
- 1 tsp coriander powder
- 1 tsp baking powder
- Salt and pepper to taste
- Oil for frying

Caramelized Onion Relish:
- 2 large onions, sliced
- 2 tbsp olive oil
- 2 tbsp balsamic vinegar
- 2 tbsp maple syrup
- Salt and pepper to taste

Instructions: Falafel

1. In a food processor, pulse the chickpeas, parsley, cilantro, garlic, onion, cumin, coriander, baking powder, salt and pepper until it forms a coarse paste.
2. Shape the mixture into small balls or patties.
3. In a deep pan, heat the oil over medium-high heat.
4. Fry the falafel in batches, until they are golden brown and crispy, about 2-3 minutes per side.

Caramelized Onion Relish:

1. In a pan, heat olive oil over medium-high heat.
2. Add the sliced onions and cook for about 10 minutes, stirring occasionally, until they are caramelized and soft.
3. Stir in the balsamic vinegar and maple syrup and cook for another 2-3 minutes, until the liquid is reduced and sticky.
4. Season with salt and pepper to taste.

SOUPS

Part Two features a range of luxurious vegan soup recipes, with a variety of flavours and textures to suit every taste. They make a perfect starter or light meal, and are sure to warm you up on a chilly day.

Gourmet Carrot and Coriander Soup with Coconut Milk

This soup is a perfect combination of sweet and savory flavors, the carrots are naturally sweet and the coconut milk and coriander give it a delicious depth of flavor. The addition of ginger also adds a nice kick of heat to the soup. This recipe is easy to make and can be served as a starter or a light meal. It can also be garnished with fresh parsley, pomegranate and sunflower seeds.

Ingredients:

- 2 tbsp coconut oil
- 1 onion, diced
- 2 cloves of garlic, minced
- 4 cups diced carrots
- 2 cups vegetable broth
- 1 can of coconut milk
- 1 tbsp grated ginger
- 2 tsp ground coriander
- Salt and pepper, to taste
- Fresh parsley, pomegranate and sunflower seeds., for garnish

Instructions:
1. In a large pot or Dutch oven, heat the coconut oil over medium heat.
2. Add the onion and garlic and sauté until translucent.
3. Add the carrots and sauté for an additional 5 minutes.
4. Pour in the vegetable broth and bring the mixture to a simmer.
5. Reduce the heat to low, cover the pot, and let simmer for 20 minutes or until the carrots are tender.
6. Remove from heat and let cool.
7. Using an immersion blender or a regular blender, puree the soup until smooth.
8. Return the pot to the heat, stir in the coconut milk, ginger, coriander, salt, and pepper.
9. Bring the mixture to a simmer and cook for an additional 5 minutes.
10. Serve hot and garnish with fresh parsley, pomegranate and sunflower seeds.

Beetroot Bliss Soup

This recipe is a true gem that combines the earthy flavor of beetroots with the sweetness of sweet potatoes, creating a velvety, nutrient-packed soup that is both comforting and satisfying. The added touch of coconut milk gives the soup a creamy, exotic flavor that complements the natural sweetness of the vegetables perfectly. This soup is not only vegan but gluten-free as well, making it a perfect choice for a range of dietary requirements. Whether you serve it as a warming starter or a satisfying main, this beetroot soup is sure to impress your taste buds and provide your body with a boost of nourishment

Ingredients:

- 4 medium-sized beetroots, peeled and chopped
- 1 large sweet potato, peeled and chopped
- 1 large onion, chopped
- 3 cloves of garlic, minced
- 4 cups of vegetable stock
- 1 can of coconut milk
- 1 tablespoon of olive oil
- 1 teaspoon of cumin
- Salt and pepper to taste

Instructions:

1. In a large pot, heat the olive oil over medium heat. Add the chopped onions and sauté until they become soft and translucent.
2. Add the minced garlic and cumin, stirring for a minute until fragrant.
3. Add the chopped beetroots and sweet potato to the pot, and stir to coat them with the onion mixture.
4. Pour the vegetable stock over the vegetables, and bring the mixture to a boil. Reduce the heat and let it simmer for about 20 minutes, until the vegetables are soft and tender.
5. Add the can of coconut milk to the pot, and blend the soup with an immersion blender until smooth.
6. Season the soup with salt and pepper to taste.

Serve the soup hot, garnished with fresh herbs, a drizzle of coconut cream, or a sprinkle of parsley

Garden Bliss Pea Soup with Mint & Lime

This recipe for Garden Bliss Pea Soup with Mint & Lime is a delicious and healthy way to enjoy the fresh flavours of spring. The combination of sweet peas and tender potatoes is enhanced by the bright and zesty flavours of mint and lime. The soup is easy to prepare and comes together in just a few simple steps. With its vibrant colour and fresh taste, this soup is perfect for a light lunch or as a starter for a larger meal. The addition of fresh mint leaves as a garnish adds a touch of colour and a burst of flavour that is sure to delight the senses.

Ingredients:

- 2 tbsp olive oil
- 1 medium onion, chopped
- 3 cloves of garlic, minced
- 2 cups fresh or frozen peas
- 3 medium potatoes, peeled and chopped
- 4 cups vegetable broth
- 1 tsp dried mint
- 1 tsp salt
- 1 tsp black pepper
- 1 lime, juiced
- Fresh mint leaves for garnish

Instructions:

1. In a large saucepan, heat the olive oil over medium heat. Add the onion and cook until soft, about 5 minutes.
2. Add the garlic and cook for another minute.
3. Add the peas, potatoes, vegetable broth, dried mint, salt and pepper. Bring the mixture to a boil, then reduce heat and let it simmer for 20 minutes.
4. Remove the soup from heat and puree with an immersion blender until smooth.
5. Stir in the lime juice and adjust seasoning as needed.
6. Serve hot, garnished with fresh mint leaves.

Rosemary Roasted Tomato Bisque with Smoked Paprika Drizzle

This recipe is a delicious and comforting soup that is perfect for any occasion. The combination of juicy and ripe tomatoes, sweet red onions, and fragrant garlic is elevated to new heights by the addition of rosemary, which provides a delightful herbal flavour. The roasted vegetables are then blended with vegetable broth to create a smooth and creamy bisque that is both healthy and satisfying. The smoked paprika drizzle adds a touch of smoky flavour and a pop of colour that makes this soup truly special.

Ingredients:

- 4 lbs ripe tomatoes, halved
- 1 large red onion, sliced
- 4 cloves garlic, minced
- 2 tbsp olive oil
- Salt and pepper, to taste
- 2 tsp dried rosemary
- 4 cups vegetable broth
- 1 tbsp smoked paprika
- 2 tbsp nutritional yeast
- 1 tsp agave syrup
- 2 tbsp freshly squeezed lemon juice

Instructions:

1. Preheat the oven to 400°F.
2. Line a baking sheet with parchment paper.
3. Arrange the tomatoes, onion and garlic on the prepared baking sheet.
4. Drizzle with olive oil, salt, pepper and dried rosemary.
5. Roast for 25-30 minutes, or until the vegetables are tender and caramelized.
6. In a blender or food processor, puree the roasted vegetables with the vegetable broth until smooth.
7. Pour the puree into a large saucepan and heat over medium heat.
8. In a small bowl, mix together the smoked paprika, nutritional yeast, agave syrup and lemon juice.
9. Stir the mixture into the soup and cook for another 5 minutes, or until heated through.
10. Serve hot and enjoy! You can also add a swirl of coconut cream or vegan sour cream on top for added richness.

Fennel's Finest: A Creamy Vegan Soup

This vegan Fennel Soup is a light and flavourful soup that is perfect for any time of year, but I particularly enjoy it on those cold rainy days here in Ireland when you are stuck indoors and long for a comforting treat. The combination of fennel, onion, and garlic creates a rich and aromatic broth that is both delicious and nutritious. The use of almond milk gives the soup a creamy texture and a nutty flavour, while the fresh fennel fronds add a touch of freshness to the soup. Whether you're looking for a healthy and satisfying meal or simply want to enjoy a comforting bowl of soup, this vegan Fennel Soup is sure to become a favourite.

Ingredients:

- 2 large fennel bulbs, sliced
- 1 large onion, chopped
- half a cup of sweetcorn
- 3 cloves of garlic, minced
- 3 tablespoons of olive oil
- 4 cups of vegetable broth
- 1 teaspoon of dried thyme
- 1 teaspoon of fennel seeds
- Salt and pepper to taste
- 1/2 cup of unsweetened almond milk
- Fresh fennel fronds for garnish or crutons

Instructions:

1. In a large pot, heat the olive oil over medium heat. Add the sliced fennel, onion, and garlic, and cook until the vegetables are soft and fragrant, about 10 minutes.
2. Stir in the dried thyme, sweetcorn, fennel seeds, salt and pepper, and cook for another minute.
3. Add the vegetable broth to the pot and bring to a boil. Reduce the heat and let the soup simmer for 20 minutes, or until the fennel is tender.
4. Remove the soup from heat and let it cool slightly.
5. In a blender, puree the soup until it is smooth.
6. Stir in the almond milk, and return the soup to the pot.
7. Reheat the soup over low heat, stirring occasionally.
8. Serve the soup hot, garnished with crutons

Earthy Elegance: Vegan Mushroom Soup

This is a hearty and flavourful soup, made from a mixture of mushrooms, onions, garlic, and seasonings. It starts with sautéing the onion and garlic in olive oil, then adding the mushrooms and cooking until they're tender. Flour is sprinkled over the mixture to thicken the soup, and then the vegetable broth is gradually poured in and simmered. The mixture is blended until smooth and then seasoned with coconut cream, nutritional yeast, salt, pepper, and lemon juice. The finished soup is served hot and garnished with parsley and chives for a touch of fresh flavour.

Ingredients:

- 2 tbsp olive oil
- 1 large onion, diced
- 4 cloves of garlic, minced
- 1 lb mixed mushrooms (such as shiitake, cremini and button), sliced
- 1 tsp dried thyme
- 1 tsp dried rosemary
- 3 tbsp all-purpose flour
- 4 cups vegetable broth
- 1 cup coconut cream
- 1 tbsp nutritional yeast
- Salt and pepper to taste
- 2 tbsp freshly squeezed lemon juice
- 2 tbsp chopped fresh parsley, for garnish
- 2 tbsp chopped fresh chives, for garnish

Instructions:

1. In a large saucepan, heat the olive oil over medium heat.
2. Add the onion and garlic and cook until softened, about 5 minutes.
3. Add the mushrooms and cook until they release their moisture and are tender, about 10 minutes.
4. Stir in the thyme and rosemary and cook for another minute.
5. Sprinkle the flour over the mushroom mixture and stir to combine.
6. Gradually pour in the broth, whisking constantly to avoid lumps.
7. Bring the mixture to a boil, then reduce heat and let it simmer for 10 minutes.
8. Remove from heat and let it cool for a few minutes.
9. Blend the mixture in a blender or with an immersion blender until smooth.
10. Return the soup to the saucepan and stir in the coconut cream and nutritional yeast.
11. Season with salt and pepper to taste.
12. Stir in the lemon juice and heat through.
13. Serve hot and garnish with parsley and chives.

Soothing Sage & Smoky Pumpkin Soup

This vegan pumpkin soup recipe showcases the flavours of fall with the combination of pumpkin, sage, and thyme. The addition of smoked paprika gives it a unique twist and depth of flavor, while the vegan cream alternative adds a rich and creamy texture. Enjoy!

Ingredients:

- 1 medium pumpkin, peeled and diced
- 1 large onion, diced
- 4 cloves of garlic, minced
- 4 cups of vegetable broth
- 1 tsp dried sage
- 1 tsp dried thyme
- 1 tsp smoked paprika
- Salt and pepper to taste
- 1/4 cup of heavy cream (vegan alternative: coconut cream)
- A handful of fresh sage leaves, chopped

Instructions:

1. In a large pot, heat a tablespoon of oil over medium heat. Add the onion and garlic and cook until soften
2. Add the diced pumpkin and continue to cook for 2-3 minutes.
3. Pour in the vegetable broth and add the dried sage, thyme, paprika, salt and pepper. Stir to combine.
4. Bring the mixture to a boil, then reduce heat and let it simmer for 20-25 minutes, or until the pumpkin is tender.
5. Using an immersion blender or a regular blender, puree the soup until smooth.
6. If desired, add a splash of heavy cream or coconut cream for added richness.
7. Serve hot, topped with a handful or pomegranate seeds and cashew crème.

PART 3

SALADS

Part Three includes a variety of beautifully crafted vegan salad recipes, perfect for any occasion. From crisp and colourful roasted eggplant and tomato salad to hearty grain-based salads, these dishes showcase the natural flavours and textures of fresh ingredients.

Strawberry and Vegan Feta Walnut Salad with Minty Balsamic Dressing

This salad is a delightful blend of sweet and tangy flavours, with the juicy strawberries, crumbled vegan feta, and crunchy walnuts providing the perfect balance of textures. The dressing is made with a balsamic vinegar base and a touch of honey, which complements the sweetness of the strawberries, while the mint leaves add a fresh and invigorating touch. A great option for a light and healthy meal or as a side dish at any gathering.

Ingredients:

- 4 cups mixed greens
- 1 cup strawberries, hulled and halved
- 1/2 cup vegan feta cheese, crumbled
- 1/2 cup toasted walnuts, roughly chopped
- 1/4 cup fresh mint leaves, chopped
- Salt and freshly ground black pepper, to taste

For the dressing:

- 2 tablespoons balsamic vinegar
- 1 tablespoon Dijon mustard
- 1 tablespoon honey (or agave syrup for vegan option)
- 4 tablespoons extra-virgin olive oil
- Salt and freshly ground black pepper, to taste

Instructions:

1. In a large bowl, combine the mixed greens, strawberries, vegan feta cheese, toasted walnuts, and mint leaves.
2. In a small bowl, whisk together the balsamic vinegar, Dijon mustard, honey, olive oil, salt, and pepper until fully combined.
3. Pour the dressing over the salad and gently toss to coat.
4. Serve immediately and enjoy the sweet, savoury, and refreshing experience!

Wild Rice and Pomegranate Salad with Pistachio Dressing

This recipe is a sophisticated and delicious vegan lunch that is packed with flavours and textures. The wild rice provides a nutty and earthy base, while the pomegranate seeds add a burst of sweetness and acidity. The pistachios add a crunchy texture and the homemade pistachio dressing adds a rich and aromatic flavour. This dish is perfect for a fancy lunch or a light dinner.

Ingredients:

- 1 cup wild rice, cooked
- 1 cup pomegranate seeds
- 1/2 cup pistachios, chopped
- 1/2 cup parsley, chopped
- 1/2 cup mint, chopped
- 1/4 cup red onion, diced
- 1/4 cup olive oil
- 2 tbsp lemon juice
- 1 tsp honey (or agave nectar for vegan version)
- 1/2 tsp salt
- 1/4 tsp black pepper
- 1/4 tsp ground cinnamon
- 1/4 tsp ground nutmeg

Instructions:

1. In a large mixing bowl, combine the cooked wild rice, pomegranate seeds, chopped pistachios, chopped parsley and mint, and diced red onion.
2. In a separate small mixing bowl, whisk together the olive oil, lemon juice, honey (or agave nectar), salt, pepper, cinnamon, and nutmeg to create the pistachio dressing.
3. Pour the dressing over the salad and toss until everything is evenly coated.
4. Serve chilled or at room temperature as a side dish or as a main course with a side of your choice.

Bountiful Broccoli, Date and Pistachio Salad

This salad is a great option for a fine-dining experience as it combines the tenderness of roasted broccoli with the sweetness of dates and the crunch of pistachios. The balsamic vinegar and olive oil dressing adds a nice tangy flavour to the salad and make it a perfect side dish.

Ingredients:

- 1 head of broccoli, cut into small florets
- 1/2 cup of dates, pitted and roughly chopped
- 1/2 cup of pistachio nuts, roughly chopped
- 2 tbsp of olive oil
- 2 tbsp of balsamic vinegar
- Salt and pepper, to taste

Instructions:

1. Preheat your oven to 375°F (190°C).
2. Spread the broccoli florets on a baking sheet and drizzle with 1 tbsp of olive oil. Season with salt and pepper.
3. Roast in the oven for about 15-20 minutes, or until the broccoli is tender and lightly browned.
4. While the broccoli is roasting, prepare the dressing. In a small bowl, whisk together the remaining 1 tbsp of olive oil, balsamic vinegar, salt and pepper.
5. Once the broccoli is done roasting, remove it from the oven and let it cool for a few minutes.
6. In a large mixing bowl, combine the cooked broccoli, chopped dates, and pistachios.
7. Toss everything together with the dressing.
8. Serve the salad on a large platter and enjoy!

Sunburst Salad.

This Sunburst Salad is a feast for the eyes and the taste buds! The juicy sweetness of the blood oranges and the vibrant yellow color of the tomatoes are balanced by the nutty crunch of the almonds and the tangy creaminess of the vegan cheese. The dressing adds a perfect balance of sweet and sour notes to bring all the flavours together. It's a perfect salad for a light lunch or dinner, and it's packed with healthy nutrients and antioxidants. Enjoy!

Ingredients:

- 2 cups of rocket leaves
- 1/2 cup of sliced almonds
- 2 yellow tomatoes, sliced
- 2 blood oranges, peeled and segmented
- Vegan cheese, crumbled or grated, for garnish

For the dressing:

- 2 tablespoons of extra-virgin olive oil
- 1 tablespoon of balsamic vinegar
- 1 tablespoon of maple syrup
- Salt and pepper to taste

Instructions:

1. Toast the sliced almonds in a dry skillet over medium heat until lightly browned and fragrant. Set aside to cool.
2. In a large mixing bowl, combine the rocket leaves, sliced yellow tomatoes, and segmented blood oranges.
3. In a small bowl, whisk together the olive oil, balsamic vinegar, maple syrup, salt, and pepper until well combined.
4. Drizzle the dressing over the salad and toss to coat the ingredients evenly.
5. Garnish the salad with crumbled or grated vegan cheese and the toasted sliced almonds.

Avocado and Heirloom Tomato Symphony

This salad is packed with fresh and healthy ingredients, and the combination of the creamy avocado with the juicy tomato, tangy red onion, and bright scallions makes for a delicious and satisfying dish. The dressing brings everything together with its bright, acidic flavor and balances the richness of the avocado. It's a great way to get your daily dose of vegetables and healthy fats all in one delicious package!

Ingredients:

- 1 ripe avocado, peeled, pitted, and diced
- 4 scallions, thinly sliced
- 2 large tomatoes, diced
- 1/2 red onion, thinly sliced
- 2 tablespoons extra-virgin olive oil
- 2 tablespoons red wine vinegar
- 1 tablespoon fresh lemon juice
- Salt and freshly ground black pepper, to taste
- 1/4 cup fresh coriander leaves, chopped (optional)

Instructions:

1. In a large bowl, combine the avocado, scallions, tomatoes, and red onion.
2. In a small bowl, whisk together the olive oil, red wine vinegar, lemon juice, salt, and pepper.
3. Pour the dressing over the avocado mixture and toss to combine.
4. If using, sprinkle cilantro on top of the salad.
5. Serve immediately and enjoy the fresh, crunchy, and flavorful experience!

Kale and Quinoa Harvest Bowl with Cherry Tomatoes, Apples, and Toasted Sunflower Seeds

This salad is a perfect combination of flavours and textures, with the hearty quinoa, crispy kale, sweet cherry tomatoes, and juicy apples providing a range of nutrients and flavour. The dressing is made with a tangy apple cider vinegar base, which complements the sweetness of the apples, while the toasted sunflower seeds add a nutty crunch. The lemon juice and parsley garnish finish off the dish with a bright, fresh touch. This bowl is a great way to celebrate the harvest and get your daily dose of greens and whole grains in one delicious and satisfying meal.

Ingredients:

- 1 cup quinoa, cooked
- 4 cups kale, chopped
- 1 cup cherry tomatoes, halved
- 1 large apple, diced
- 2 tablespoons sunflower seeds, toasted
- Salt and freshly ground black pepper, to taste

For the dressing:

- 2 tablespoons apple cider vinegar
- 1 tablespoon Dijon mustard
- 1 tablespoon maple syrup (or agave syrup for vegan option)
- 4 tablespoons extra-virgin olive oil
- Salt and freshly ground black pepper, to taste

Garnish:

- Fresh lemon juice
- Fresh parsley leaves, chopped

Instructions:

1. In a large bowl, combine the cooked quinoa, chopped kale, cherry tomatoes, diced apple, and toasted sunflower seeds.
2. In a small bowl, whisk together the apple cider vinegar, Dijon mustard, maple syrup, olive oil, salt, and pepper until fully combined.
3. Pour the dressing over the salad and gently toss to coat.
4. Squeeze a little lemon juice over the top and sprinkle with chopped parsley.
5. Serve immediately and enjoy the delicious and wholesome meal!

Roasted Garlic and Lemon Vegan Hummus

This vegan hummus is a creamy and flavourful dip, made with chickpeas and tahini, and seasoned with lemon juice and freshly ground black pepper. The roasted garlic adds a rich and savoury depth of flavour, while the olive oil provides a smooth and creamy texture. The paprika, parsley, and pine nut garnish give the hummus a touch of colour and nuttiness, making it a perfect snack or appetizer for any gathering.

Ingredients:

- 1 can chickpeas, drained and rinsed
- 2 cloves garlic, roasted
- 2 tablespoons tahini
- 2 tablespoons extra-virgin olive oil
- 2 tablespoons lemon juice
- Salt and freshly ground black pepper, to taste
- 1/4 teaspoon paprika, for garnish
- 1 tablespoon chopped fresh parsley, for garnish
- 1 tablespoon toasted pine nuts, for garnish

Instructions:

1. In a food processor, combine the chickpeas, roasted garlic, tahini, olive oil, lemon juice, salt, and pepper.
2. Process until smooth and creamy.
3. Transfer the hummus to a serving dish and smooth the top with a spatula.
4. Place in the centre of a dish and garnish with baby tomatoes, radicchio and rocket. Drizzle with Oilve oil.

Amazing Avocado, Rocket, and Roasted Red Pepper Salad with Walnut Vinaigrette

This salad is a fresh and colourful mix of ingredients. The creamy avocado and the crisp rocket leaves provide a contrast of textures, while the sweet and smoky roasted red pepper and the tangy red onion add depth and complexity to the dish. The walnut vinaigrette, made with red wine vinegar and Dijon mustard, brings everything together with its nutty and acidic flavor, making it a perfect complement to the richness of the avocado. This salad is a great way to get your daily dose of greens, healthy fats, and antioxidants, all in one delicious and elegant dish.

Ingredients:

- 2 ripe avocados, peeled, pitted, and diced
- 4 cups rocket (arugula) leaves, washed and dried
- 1 roasted red pepper, diced
- 1/2 red onion, thinly sliced
- 1/2 cup walnuts, toasted and roughly chopped
- Salt and freshly ground black pepper, to taste

For the vinaigrette:

- 2 tablespoons red wine vinegar
- 1 tablespoon Dijon mustard
- 2 tablespoons extra-virgin olive oil
- Salt and freshly ground black pepper, to taste

Instructions:

1. In a large bowl, combine the diced avocado, rocket leaves, diced roasted red pepper, sliced red onion, and toasted walnuts.
2. In a small bowl, whisk together the red wine vinegar, Dijon mustard, olive oil, salt, and pepper until fully combined.
3. Drizzle the vinaigrette over the salad and gently toss to coat.
4. Season the salad with additional salt and pepper, if needed.
5. Serve immediately and enjoy the delicious and sophisticated flavor!

PART 4

DESSERTS & SWEETS

Part Four features a variety of exquisite vegan dessert recipes, including creamy cheesecakes, delicate pastries, and fresh fruit tarts. These delicious treats showcase the finesse and creativity of plant-based cooking, and are the perfect end to any gourmet vegan meal.

Coffee-Coconut Tiramisu Delight

The Coffee-Coconut Tiramisu Delight is a vegan twist on the classic Italian dessert, featuring rich and creamy layers of aquafaba and coconut cream. The addition of coffee and cocoa powder adds a bold flavour, while rum (optional) adds a hint of warmth. Ladyfingers soaked in coffee and cocoa complement the creamy mixture, making this both vegan and dairy-free, suitable for those with dietary restrictions. Serve chilled and garnished with toasted coconut flakes. A unique and delicious treat, easy to make with just a few simple ingredients. Enjoy with a cup of coffee!

Ingredients:

- 2 cups of aquafaba (liquid from a can of chickpeas)
- 1 cup powdered sugar
- 1 tsp vanilla extract
- 1 cup coconut cream
- 1/2 cup strong coffee
- 1/4 cup cocoa powder
- 1 tbsp rum (optional)
- Vegan ladyfingers
- Toasted coconut flakes for garnish

Instructions:

1. In a large bowl, beat aquafaba with an electric mixer until stiff peaks form.
2. Gradually add in the powdered sugar and vanilla extract, continue beating until mixture is glossy and holds stiff peaks.
3. In a separate bowl, whisk together the coconut cream, coffee, cocoa powder, and rum (if using) until well combined.
4. Gently fold the coconut mixture into the aquafaba mixture until well combined.
5. In a 9-inch square dish, layer half the ladyfingers on the bottom and then spread half the coconut mixture on top. Repeat this process with the remaining ladyfingers and coconut mixture.
6. Cover and refrigerate for at least 2 hours, or overnight.
7. If you fancy, sprinkle toasted coconut flakes on top.

Enjoy your unique and delicious vegan tiramisu twist!

Deconstructed Eton Mess

The Deconstructed Eton Mess is a vegan take on the classic British dessert. Featuring fresh berries, vegan meringue made with aquafaba, vegan whipped cream made with coconut cream, and chopped pistachios, this dessert is both delicious and dairy-free. The berry puree is thickened with agave syrup, vanilla extract, and a pinch of salt, creating the perfect sauce for this dessert. Simply layer the berry puree, vegan meringue, and vegan whipped cream in a glass or bowl, and enjoy this tasty and unique twist on a classic.

Ingredients:

- 2 cups of fresh berries (strawberries, raspberries, and blueberries)
- 1/2 cup of vegan meringue (made with aquafaba)
- 1/2 cup of vegan whipped cream (made with coconut cream)
- 1/4 cup of chopped pistachios
- 2 tablespoons of agave syrup
- 1 teaspoon of vanilla extract
- Pinch of salt

Instructions:

1. Preheat the oven to 200°F.
2. In a food processor, blend the berries until smooth and strain through a fine-mesh sieve to remove any seeds.
3. In a small saucepan, heat the berry puree with agave syrup, vanilla extract, and a pinch of salt over medium heat. Cook for about 5 minutes, or until the puree thickens slightly.
4. Remove from heat and let it cool.
5. In a large bowl, whisk the aquafaba until stiff peaks form. Fold in the chopped pistachios.
6. In a separate bowl, whip the coconut cream until stiff peaks form.
7. To assemble, place spoonfuls of the berry puree, vegan meringue, and vegan whipped cream into a glass or bowl. Repeat the layers, making sure to end with a layer of whipped cream.
8. Garnish with additional chopped pistachios and berries, if desired.
9. Serve immediately or chill in the refrigerator for 1 hour before serving.

Raspberry-Coconut Chia Parfait

This dish is not only delicious and healthy, but also easy to make, and can be served as a perfect breakfast or brunch option for a vegan diet. With the combination of sweet raspberries and coconut milk, nutty chia seeds, and crunchy walnuts, it is a perfect balance of flavors and textures that will surely wake up your taste buds. The dish is named "Raspberry-Coconut Chia Parfait" and it is a sophisticated and elegant breakfast dish that is perfect for special occasions or for a weekend treat.

Ingredients:

- 1 cup raspberries
- 1/2 cup coconut milk
- 1/4 cup chia seeds
- 2 tbsp maple syrup
- 1 tsp vanilla extract
- 1/4 tsp salt
- 1/4 cup shredded coconut
- 1/4 cup chopped walnuts
- 1 ripe banana, sliced

Instructions:

1. In a small saucepan over medium heat, combine the raspberries, coconut milk, maple syrup, vanilla extract, and salt. Stir frequently until the raspberries break down and the mixture thickens, about 10 minutes. Remove from heat and let it cool.
2. In a medium bowl, mix together the chia seeds, shredded coconut, and chopped walnuts.
3. In a jar or glass, layer the raspberry mixture, chia seed mixture, and banana slices, starting and ending with the raspberry mixture.
4. Cover and refrigerate overnight or at least 2 hours.
5. Enjoy your delicious and nutritious vegan breakfast parfait.

Note: You can also add any other fruits of your choice or granola for added crunch.

Silken Strawberry Vegan Ice Cream

Silken Strawberry Vegan Ice Cream is a delicious and creamy treat that's perfect for those who are looking for a vegan alternative to traditional ice cream. Made with raw cashews and coconut milk, this ice cream is rich and indulgent, yet it's also dairy-free and vegan-friendly. The addition of strawberries and vanilla bean paste give it a sweet and fruity flavour, while the agave syrup and lemon juice add a touch of brightness. Whether you're in the mood for a sweet snack or a dessert, this vegan ice cream is sure to satisfy your cravings and leave you feeling refreshed and satisfied.

Ingredients:

2 cups raw cashews, soaked overnight
2 cups full-fat coconut milk
1 cup freshly pureed strawberries
1 cup agave syrup
2 tbsp. lemon juice
1 tsp. pure vanilla extract
1 pinch of salt

Instructions:

1. Drain and rinse the soaked cashews and add them to a high-speed blender with the coconut milk. Blend until silky smooth.
2. Add the freshly pureed strawberries, agave syrup, lemon juice, vanilla extract, and a pinch of salt. Blend again until everything is well combined.
3. Pour the mixture into an ice cream maker and churn according to the manufacturer's instructions until the ice cream reaches a creamy and soft-serve consistency.
4. Transfer the ice cream to a freezer-safe container and freeze for at least 6 hours, or until firm.
5. Before serving, remove the ice cream from the freezer and allow it to sit at room temperature for 10 minutes to soften slightly.
6. Scoop the ice cream into bowls or cones and enjoy the burst of fresh strawberry flavour in every bite!

Poached Perfection: Vegan Plum Delight

This recipe is a unique take on the classic poached plums, which is a sophisticated and delicious vegan dish that will be perfect for any fine dining occasion. The technique of poaching fruit is used by many Michelin star chefs as it helps to enhance the natural sweetness and flavor of the fruit. The red wine and spices also add an extra layer of complexity to the dish. The recipe can be accompanied by a vegan vanilla ice cream which will add a creamy texture to the dish.

Ingredients:

- 2 lbs plums, halved and pitted
- 2 cups red wine
- 1 cup sugar
- 2 cinnamon sticks
- 2 star anise
- 2 sprigs thyme
- 1 vanilla bean, split and scraped
- 1 tbsp cornstarch
- 1 tbsp water
- Vegan vanilla ice cream, to serve

Instructions:

1. In a large saucepan, combine the red wine, sugar, cinnamon sticks, star anise, thyme, and vanilla bean. Bring to a simmer over medium heat, stirring until the sugar has dissolved.
2. Add the plums to the pan and bring to a simmer. Reduce the heat to low and cover with a lid. Gently poach the plums for 15-20 minutes or until tender.
3. In a small bowl, whisk together the cornstarch and water to make a slurry. Stir the slurry into the pan and continue to simmer for a further 2-3 minutes, or until the sauce thickens.
4. Remove the pan from heat and let the plums cool down. Remove the cinnamon sticks, star anise, thyme and vanilla bean.
5. To serve, spoon the poached plums and their sauce over vegan vanilla ice cream.

.

Strawberry Sensation Bowl

This is a delightful dessert that combines the sweetness of fresh strawberries and honey with the nutritious goodness of almond milk and protein powder. The addition of chia seeds and cinnamon makes this smoothie bowl even more nutritious, while the toppings of almond granola, coconut flakes, and sliced strawberries add a delightful crunch to every bite. With its perfect balance of sweetness, texture, and flavour, the Strawberry Sensation Bowl is sure to become your go-to dessert whenever you want to indulge in something delicious and healthy.

Ingredients:

1 cup fresh strawberries
1 banana
1 cup almond milk
1 scoop vanilla protein powder
1 tsp honey
1 tsp vanilla extract 1/2 tsp cinnamon 1 tbsp chia seeds

Toppings: Fresh strawberries, sliced Almond, granola, Coconut flakes, maple syrup

Instructions:

1. In a blender, add the strawberries, banana, almond milk, protein powder, honey, vanilla extract, and cinnamon. Blend until smooth.
2. Stir in the chia seeds and let the mixture sit for 5 minutes to thicken.
3. Pour the mixture into a bowl and top with fresh strawberries, almond granola, coconut flakes, and a drizzle of maple syrup
4. You can also add frozen fruit to the mixture for a thicker consistency. You can also use any type of milk you prefer, such as soy milk or oat milk.
5. Decorate with sliced strawberries, a sprig of mint, grated coconut or cashews and edible flowers.

PART 5

.

CAKES & LOAFS

Part Four includes a range of decadent vegan cake and loaf recipes. From rich and moist chocolate cakes to sweet and tender fruit loaves, these desserts are perfect for any special occasion or just as a sweet treat. These recipes showcase the versatility of plant-based ingredients and prove that vegan baking can be just as delicious as its traditional counterpart.

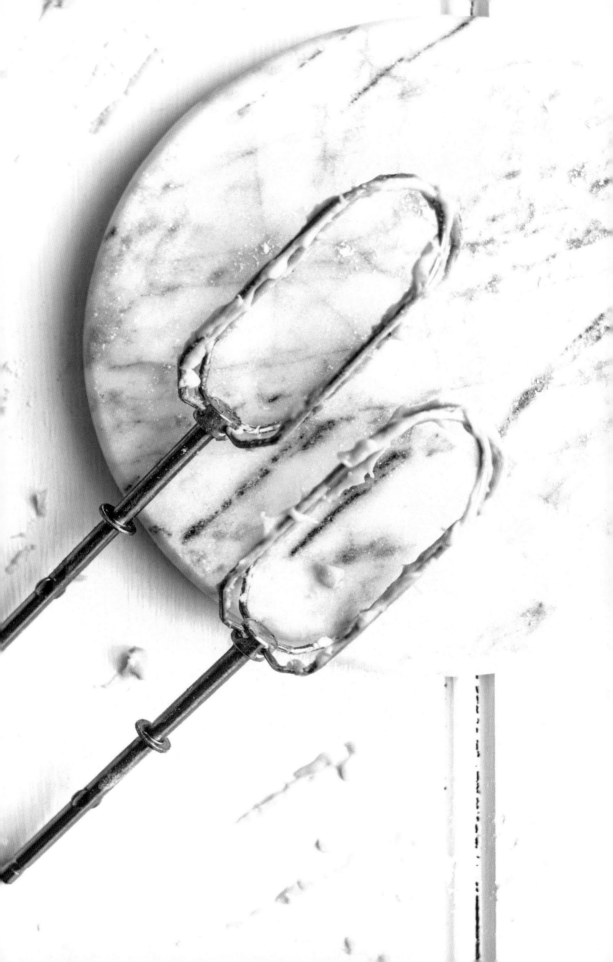

Deconstructed Apple Fritter Tart

This recipe features techniques commonly used by Michelin star chefs, such as the use of seasonal ingredients and layering flavours. The "deconstructed" aspect of the dish adds a unique twist to the traditional apple fritter recipe, making it visually striking and tasty.

Ingredients:

- 2 cups all-purpose flour
- 2 tsp baking powder
- 1/2 tsp salt
- 1/2 cup vegan butter, chilled and diced
- 1/2 cup cold plant based milk
- 1/2 cup granulated sugar
- 1 tbsp ground cinnamon
- 1 tsp vanilla extract
- 3 cups thinly sliced and peeled Granny Smith apples
- 1/4 cup maple syrup
- 1/4 cup vegan cream cheese. (I recommend Philadelphia Cream Cheese Plant-Based or Violife Plain Cream Cheese)
- Powdered sugar for dusting

Directions:

1. Preheat oven to 350°F. Grease a 9-inch round tart pan with non-stick cooking spray.
2. In a large mixing bowl, combine flour, baking powder, and salt. Using your fingers or a pastry cutter, work in the chilled vegan butter until the mixture resembles coarse crumbs.
3. Stir in the cold vegan milk, 1/4 cup granulated sugar, 1/2 tablespoon cinnamon, and vanilla extract until a dough forms.
4. Press the dough into the prepared tart pan, creating a 1/4-inch thick crust.
5. In a separate mixing bowl, toss the sliced apples with the remaining 1/4 cup granulated sugar and 1/2 tablespoon cinnamon.
6. Arrange the apple slices in concentric circles on top of the crust, leaving a 1-inch border around the edges.
7. Drizzle the maple syrup over the apples.
8. In a small mixing bowl, combine the vegan cream cheese, 1 tablespoon maple syrup, and a pinch of cinnamon. Spread the mixture over the apples.
9. Bake for 45-50 minutes, or until the crust is golden brown and the apples are tender.
10. Let the tart cool for 10 minutes before removing it from the pan. Dust with powdered sugar before serving.

Lemon Blueberry Burst Cheesecake with Almond Crust

This recipe is for a Lemon Blueberry Burst Cheesecake with Almond Crust. Made with almond flour, coconut oil, maple syrup, lemon juice and blueberries to garnish. The crust is baked, then a mixture of pureed tofu and lemon is added, and finally a blueberry mixture is poured over the cheesecake. The cheesecake is refrigerated for 2 hours before serving. Enjoy the tangy and sweet flavour combination of lemon and blueberries in this delicious cheesecake.

Ingredients:

- 1 1/2 cups almond flour
- 1/4 cup melted coconut oil
- 3 tbsp maple syrup
- 1 tsp vanilla extract
- 1 block of firm tofu
- 1/2 cup coconut cream
- 1/4 cup lemon juice
- 1/4 cup lemon zest
- 1/2 cup blueberries
- 1 tbsp cornstarch
- 2 tbsp maple syrup
- 2 tbsp lemon juice
- 1 tbsp vanilla extract

Instructions:

1. Preheat oven to 350°F (175°C)
2. In a mixing bowl, combine almond flour, melted coconut oil, 3 tbsp maple syrup, and 1 tsp vanilla extract. Mix well.
3. Press mixture into bottom of 9-inch springform pan. Bake for 10-12 minutes.
4. In a blender or food processor, puree tofu, coconut cream, 1/4 cup lemon juice, and 1/4 cup lemon zest until smooth. Add a dash of yellow food colouring if you wish.
5. Pour mixture over baked crust. Bake for 20-25 minutes.
6. In a small saucepan, combine blueberries, cornstarch, 2 tbsp maple syrup, 2 tbsp lemon juice, and 1 tbsp vanilla extract. Cook over medium heat until thickened, about 5 minutes.
7. Pour blueberry mixture over baked cheesecake. Refrigerate for 2 hours.
8. Serve chilled and enjoy!

Lavender & Blueberry Truffle Tartlets

This Lavender & Blueberry Truffle Tartlet recipe is a treat for the taste buds. The crust, made from vegan graham crackers, melted vegan butter, and dried lavender, provides a delightful base for the filling. The filling, made with melted vegan dark chocolate mixed with blueberry syrup and powdered sugar, is rich, sweet, and bursting with flavour. The tartlets are garnished with edible flowers, adding a touch of elegance to the final product. With a unique combination of flavours, this vegan recipe is perfect for any special occasion or just a sweet treat.

Ingredients:

- 1 1/2 cups vegan graham cracker crumbs
- 1/3 cup vegan butter, melted
- 1 tbsp granulated sugar
- 2 tbsp dried lavender
- 1 cup blueberries
- 1 cup vegan dark chocolate chips
- 1 cup vegan heavy cream (I recommend Biona Organic Coconut Whipping Cream)
- 2 tbsp powdered sugar
- Edible flowers for garnish

Instructions:

1. Preheat oven to 350°F.
2. In a mixing bowl, combine graham cracker crumbs, melted butter, granulated sugar, and dried lavender.
3. Press mixture into mini tartlet pans. Bake for 8-10 minutes. Let cool.
4. In a saucepan, heat blueberries and 2 tbsp water until they form a syrup. Set aside to cool.
5. In a saucepan melt chocolate chips and vegan cream together until smooth. Let cool.
6. In a mixing bowl, whisk together blueberry syrup and powdered sugar. Fold in melted chocolate mixture.
7. Pour mixture into cooled crusts. Chill in the refrigerator for at least 2 hours.
8. Garnish with edible flowers before serving. Enjoy!

Lemon Lush Vegan Cake

This vegan lemon cake is a light and refreshing dessert that is perfect for any occasion. The use of vegan butter and applesauce in the batter adds a rich, creamy texture while the lemon zest and juice provide a tangy, zesty flavor. The vegan glaze on top adds a nice sweetness and a lovely shine to the cake.

Ingredients:

- 2 cups all-purpose flour
- 1 cup granulated sugar
- 1 tsp baking powder
- 1/2 tsp baking soda
- 1/2 tsp salt
- 1/2 cup vegan margarine (I recommend Kerrymaid Premium Baking Margarine)
- 1/2 cup unsweetened applesauce
- 2 tbsp grated lemon zest
- 1/4 cup fresh lemon juice
- 1 tsp vanilla extract
- 1 cup unsweetened almond milk
- 2 tbsp cornstarch

Directions:

1. Preheat oven to 350F. Grease and flour a 9-inch round cake pan.
2. In a large mixing bowl, combine flour, sugar, baking powder, baking soda, and salt.
3. In a separate mixing bowl, beat vegan baking margarine, applesauce, lemon zest, lemon juice, and vanilla extract until well combined.
4. In a small bowl, mix together the almond milk and cornstarch until smooth.
5. Slowly add the wet ingredients to the dry ingredients, alternating with the milk and cornstarch mixture. Mix until just combined.
6. Pour the batter into the prepared pan and bake for 25-30 minutes, or until a toothpick inserted into the centre comes out clean.
7. Remove the cake from the oven and let it cool completely in the pan before removing it from the pan.
8. To make the glaze, whisk together powdered sugar and lemon juice in a small bowl until smooth.
9. Drizzle the glaze over the cooled cake or if you prefer, sprinkle the icing sugar over the cake for a sweet alternative.

Choco-Citrus Avocado Dream

The Choco-Citrus Avocado Dream is a wonderful vegan dessert that is not only delicious, but also healthy. Made with fresh avocado, dates, cocoa powder, lemon juice and zest, coconut cream, vanilla extract, and cherries, this dessert is rich in flavor and packed with nutritious ingredients. Perfect for vegans who are looking for a sweet treat that won't break their dietary restrictions, this Choco-Citrus Avocado Dream is a must-try!

Ingredients:

1 ripe avocado
1 cup pitted dates
1/2 cup unsweetened cocoa powder
1 tbsp lemon juice
1 tsp lemon zest
1 cup coconut cream
1 tsp vanilla extract
1/4 cup sugar
1 cup fresh cherries, pitted and halved

Instructions:

In a food processor, blend avocado, dates, cocoa powder, lemon juice, and lemon zest until smooth.

Pour mixture into a 9-inch pie dish and freeze for 30 minutes. In a separate bowl, whisk together the coconut cream, vanilla extract, and sugar until thick and creamy.

Remove the avocado mixture from the freezer and spread the coconut cream mixture evenly over it.

Top with fresh cherries or blueberries and freeze for another hour. Let thaw for 10 minutes before serving.

Enjoy your unique and delicious vegan dessert!

Deconstructed Raspberry Dream Vegan Cheesecake

The Deconstructed Raspberry Dream Vegan Cheesecake is a wonderful and decadent dessert that is perfect for vegans. Topped with fresh raspberries and a drizzle of raspberry jam, this cheesecake is a sweet treat that will delight vegans and non-vegans alike. It's the perfect dessert for special occasions, or for a delicious and healthy indulgence.

Crust:
- 1 1/2 cups graham cracker crumbs
- 1/2 cup vegan butter, melted
- 2 tablespoons granulated sugar

Filling:
- 2 cups raw cashews, soaked in water overnight
- 1/2 cup fresh raspberries
- 1/2 cup full-fat coconut milk
- 1/2 cup maple syrup
- 1/4 cup fresh lemon juice
- 1/4 cup melted coconut oil
- 1 teaspoon vanilla extract

Topping:
- 1 cup fresh raspberries
- 1/4 cup raspberry jam
- 1 teaspoon powdered sugar (optional)

Instructions:

1. Preheat the oven to 350°F (175°C).
2. For the crust, mix together the graham cracker crumbs, melted vegan butter, and sugar in a medium bowl until well combined. Press the mixture into the bottom of a 9-inch springform pan, pressing it firmly and evenly across the bottom.
3. For the filling, drain and rinse the soaked cashews and add them to a high-speed blender or food processor. Add in the raspberries, coconut milk, maple syrup, lemon juice, melted coconut oil, and vanilla extract. Blend until the mixture is smooth and creamy.
4. Pour the filling over the crust and smooth it out evenly with a spatula.
5. For the topping, place the fresh raspberries on top of the cheesecake filling. In a small saucepan, heat the raspberry jam over low heat until it becomes a thick consistency. Drizzle the jam over the raspberries.
6. Bake the cheesecake for 25-30 minutes or until the edges are golden brown. Let it cool completely before removing from the springform pan.
7. Once cooled, refrigerate for at least 2 hours before slicing and serving.

Deconstructed Vegan Apple Tart

This recipe uses techniques like pleating the dough and using almond flour to add a sophisticated and unique twist to the traditional apple tart. The addition of spices and pecans gives it a deeper flavour and added texture. Enjoy your Deconstructed Vegan Aapple Tart!

Ingredients:

- 1 cup all-purpose flour
- 1/2 cup almond flour
- 1/4 cup coconut sugar
- 1/4 cup vegan butter, chilled and diced (I recommend Flora Plant B+tter)
- 1 tsp vanilla extract
- 1 tsp apple cider vinegar
- 1/4 tsp salt
- 1 cup peeled and diced apples
- 1/4 cup maple syrup
- 1 tbsp cornstarch
- 1 tsp lemon juice
- 1 tsp ground cinnamon
- Pinch of ground nutmeg
- 1/4 cup chopped pecans

Instructions:

1. In a large mixing bowl, combine the all-purpose flour, almond flour, coconut sugar, vegan butter, vanilla extract, apple cider vinegar, and salt. Mix until the dough comes together and forms a ball. Flatten the dough into a disk, wrap it in plastic wrap, and refrigerate for at least 1 hour.
2. In a separate mixing bowl, combine the diced apples, maple syrup, cornstarch, lemon juice, ground cinnamon, and ground nutmeg. Mix well and set aside.
3. Preheat the oven to 375F (190C). Grease a 9-inch (23cm) tart pan.
4. Roll out the chilled dough on a lightly floured surface to a thickness of 1/4 inch (0.6cm). Carefully transfer the dough to the prepared tart pan, pressing it into the bottom and up the sides.
5. Spread the apple mixture over the dough in the pan, leaving a 1-inch (2.5cm) border around the edge.
6. Sprinkle the chopped pecans over the apples.
7. Fold the edges of the dough up and over the apples, pleating the dough as needed.
8. Bake the tart for 35-40 minutes, or until the crust is golden brown and the apples are bubbly. Dust with powdered sugar or cinnamon before serving according to your tastes.

Gourmet Green Goddess Courgette Cake

This is a wonderful and delicious dessert that is perfect for vegans. Made with grated courgettes, almond flour, cocoa powder, coconut oil, and flax eggs, this cake is not only vegan, but also healthy and nutritious. The addition of maple syrup, vanilla extract, and cinnamon give this cake a rich and sweet flavor, while the chopped pecans add a crunchy texture. Whether you're looking for a dessert for a special occasion or just want a healthy treat, the Gourmet Green Goddess Courgette Cake is a must-try.

Ingredients:

- 2 cups grated courgettes
- 1 cup almond flour
- 1 cup all-purpose flour
- 1/2 cup unsweetened cocoa powder
- 1/2 cup maple syrup
- 1/2 cup melted coconut oil
- 2 flax eggs (2 tbsp ground flaxseed mixed with 6 tbsp water)
- 1 tsp vanilla extract
- 1 tsp baking powder
- 1 tsp baking soda
- 1 tsp cinnamon
- Pinch of salt
- 1/2 cup chopped pecans

Instructions:

1. Preheat the oven to 350°F (180°C). Grease and line a 9-inch (23 cm) round cake tin with parchment paper.
2. In a large bowl, mix together the grated courgettes, almond flour, all-purpose flour, cocoa powder, maple syrup, melted coconut oil, flax eggs, vanilla extract, baking powder, baking soda, cinnamon, and salt.
3. Fold in the chopped pecans.
4. Pour the batter into the prepared cake tin and smooth the top with a spatula.
5. Bake in the preheated oven for 40-45 minutes, or until a toothpick inserted into the centre comes out clean. Allow the cake to cool completely in the tin before removing and slicing.
6. Serve with a dollop of vegan whipped cream or a grated vegan chocolate (I recommend Rococo Vegan chocolate or Booja-Booja).

Captivating Carrot Cake

The Captivating Carrot Cake is a unique twist on a classic dessert, offering a delicious blend of spices and flavors, including grated carrots, chopped pecans, and raisins. Topped with a creamy vegan cream cheese frosting, this cake is sure to impress.

Ingredients:

- 2 cups all-purpose flour
- 2 tsp baking powder
- 1 tsp baking soda
- 2 tsp ground cinnamon
- 1/2 tsp ground nutmeg
- 1/2 tsp ground ginger
- 1/4 tsp ground allspice
- 1/4 tsp ground cloves
- 1/2 tsp salt
- 1 cup granulated sugar
- 1 cup unsweetened applesauce
- 1/2 cup vegetable oil
- 3 cups grated carrots
- 1 cup chopped pecans
- 1/2 cup raisins

Cream Cheese Frosting:
- 8 oz vegan cream cheese
- 1/2 cup vegan butter ((recommend Flora Plant B+tter)
- 1 tsp vanilla extract
- 2 cups powdered sugar

Instructions:

1. Preheat the oven to 350°F. Grease and flour a 9-inch round cake pan.
2. In a medium bowl, whisk together the flour, baking powder, baking soda, spices, and salt.
3. In a large mixing bowl, beat together the sugar, applesauce, and oil until smooth.

Stir in the grated carrots, pecans, and raisins.

1. Gradually add the dry ingredients to the wet ingredients until combined.
2. Pour the batter into the prepared cake pan and smooth out the top.
3. Bake for 40-50 minutes, or until a toothpick inserted into the centre comes out clean.
4. Allow the cake to cool completely before frosting.
5. To make the cream cheese frosting, beat together the vegan cream cheese, vegan butter, and vanilla extract until smooth. Gradually add the powdered sugar.
6. Once the cake has cooled, frost the top and sides of the cake with the frosting.

Bewitching Blueberry Cheesecake

This Bewitching Blueberry Cheesecake is a great dessert that is vegan, dairy-free, and gluten-free. The combination of the crunchy graham cracker crust, creamy and tangy blueberry filling, and sweet blueberry topping makes it a delicious treat for any occasion

Ingredients:

Crust: 1 1/2 cups vegan graham crackers, crushed
1/4 cup melted vegan butter
1/4 cup granulated sugar
1 tsp lemon zest

Filling:

2 cups raw cashews, soaked overnight
1 cup fresh blueberries
1/2 cup coconut cream
1/2 cup maple syrup
1/4 cup fresh lemon juice
1/4 cup melted coconut oil
1 tsp vanilla extract

Topping:
1 cup fresh blueberries
1/4 cup blueberry preserve
1 tbsp powdered sugar (optional)

Instructions:
Preheat the oven to 350°F (175°C).

For the crust, mix together the graham crackers, melted vegan butter, sugar, and lemon zest in a medium bowl until well combined. Press the mixture into the bottom of a 9-inch springform pan, making sure it's evenly distributed.

For the filling, drain and rinse the soaked cashews and add them to a high-speed blender or food processor. Add in the blueberries, coconut cream, maple syrup, lemon juice, melted coconut oil, and vanilla extract. Blend until the mixture is smooth and creamy. Pour the filling over the crust and smooth out the top with a spatula.

For the topping, place the fresh blueberries on top of the cheesecake filling. In a small saucepan, heat the blueberry preserve over low heat until it becomes a thick consistency. Drizzle the preserve over the blueberries.

Optional: sprinkle powdered sugar over the top of the cheesecake. Bake the cheesecake for 25-30 minutes or until the edges are golden brown. Let it cool completely before removing from the springform pan. Once cooled, refrigerate for at least 2 hours before slicing and serving.

And with that, the journey through the world of vegan gourmet cuisine comes to an end. I hope you enjoyed the recipes and found inspiration in each and every one of them. These dishes showcase the incredible versatility and flavor that can be found in plant-based ingredients, and demonstrate how a vegan diet can be both delicious and satisfying. Whether you are a seasoned vegan or just looking to add some more plant-based options to your diet, these recipes are sure to impress and delight. So go ahead, gather your ingredients, and get cooking.

Bon appétit!

Georgina

Printed in Great Britain
by Amazon

84c202fb-5dc2-4978-9e18-6ece2c55d02bR01